Mary's Memories

NURSING IN JURA FROM 1963-93

Mary Keith RGN SCM

Copyright © Mary Keith 2010

All rights reserved. No part of this publication may be reproduced or transmitted in any form or by any means, electronic or -mechanical including photocopying, recording or any information storage or retrieval system, without prior -permission in writing from the publisher.

First published in the United Kingdom in 2010 by
Toolbox Press

ISBN 978-0-9560084-1-1

Printed in Great Britain

Contents

Foreword	4
Starting out	5
An illustrious client	8
My own maternity experience	10
Working all hours	13
Babies galore!	15
Bella	19
All in a day's work ...	22
A ceilidh to remember	29
List of colleagues	32
Acknowledgements	33
Postscript	34

Foreword

I became Jura's resident nurse back in 1963, and continued in that role for 30 years until late 1993. As I reminisced over the challenges I had to face during that time, and the many changes that have taken place on the island, it seemed only fair to set some of it down so that others could see what it was like.

I came to live on Jura when I got married in 1959, never thinking that I would ever be nursing here.

How wrong I was!

Starting out

My career on Jura started with a phone call.

It was in 1962, when I was pregnant with my second baby, that a Dr Allan phoned from Oban to ask if I would consider being part-time nurse for the island after the birth. The doctor had been trying to find a nurse and thought that this would be a good opportunity, as I was by that time fully qualified. There had been no nurse on the island for thirty years; midwives had helped out in the past, but they had not been employed as such.

When Gordon was six months old, therefore, the Nursing Officer came to see me at home for my interview. She was, as you might say, a very *severe* person. She looked at the two children and immediately declared *"Out of the question – the children are too young!"* So I told her that Dr. Allan had asked me knowing full well that I was pregnant, after which no more was said, and I duly started my triple duties on the tenth of June 1963.

Mary as a young nurse

On my first day I went on rounds with the doctor. My first patient was an eighty-nine year old lady, and I was told that I would either be welcomed with open arms or the door would be shut in my face! However, as luck would have it, my patient knew my great-grandparents, who belonged to Jura, so I was accepted, and she was a good patient ever after.

From the beginning I always enjoyed looking after my patients, both adults and children. Speaking of children, I had, on commencement, no fewer than thirty-one children on the register, from birth to school age. Later, sadly, when I had been in post for eleven years, the health board transferred the health visiting to Islay, to one Mrs McKenzie, as by then we only had a few children.

I also had thirty adult patients, a lot of whom were elderly. At Inverlussa at that time every house was occupied; likewise at Tarbert, Knockrome and Ardmenish. At that time I had no transport as I did not drive, so I had to hire Charlie McLean, Dan Macdougall or Dougie Buie to take me about the island. It was not until 1966 that I was given my first car, which was a Hillman Imp. I had taken lessons in Greenock, and I took my driving test in Jura.

I also, at first, had no phone; this and the answerphone were put in later.

An illustrious client

During the first days, while I was still waiting for my equipment to arrive, out of the blue I had a phone call from one of the lairds. He asked me to attend to his wife, as she was threatening a miscarriage, and their own private specialists were stranded in Tayvallich by the weather. I told the laird that I was a health board nurse and not a private one, and that I would have to speak to our (relief) doctor first. *"I might not be quick on my legs, but my brain is still active"* declared the doctor (then in his eighties!) The doctor agreed to our involvement, so I set off up the island. I was to take all my instructions from the specialists, so I made my way up to Tarbert by hiring Charlie. I was in a bit of a dilemma, as my equipment had still not arrived; however, I borrowed a stethoscope and blood pressure apparatus from the doctor.

The lady laird was very nice, offering her nanny's services to look after my children should I have to stay overnight; however, in the event that was not required, as Dr Bonner managed to come across and take over from me.

He was stranded on Jura for another three days before he made it back to the mainland! He later phoned and thanked me for my help. The situation had been saved, and, on a subsequent holiday, the lady laird introduced me to her baby.

While I was looking after her, reporters and photographers had been following me, trying to get a picture, which I declined, and asking me for details, right down to what kind of wallpaper was on the walls. I replied that I was there to look after the patient, not to look at my surroundings! They even wanted to know what drugs were given, but I replied that they would have to speak to her doctor for that. They were very persistent, even coming to my home and the house where I was seeing another patient, where, fortunately, Charlie stopped them. A small article went into the paper subsequently about me attending to the lady laird, and I still have the cutting to this day.

My own maternity experience

The reason I am going to tell you about the next episode is to let you know how difficult it was in those days to have a baby on the island. This is my own experience, going back to before I became Jura's nurse and midwife.

When I was in labour with my first child, on the second of January 1961, my membranes ruptured at 6am. We did not, at that point, have a nurse working on the island, and so the doctor had sole responsibility for the case. As the baby was in the breech position, I was worried, as, being a trained midwife as well as a nurse, I knew of the complications there could be; therefore the doctor was called, but nothing was done. At 1pm he was called again as I had severe back pain. I was told that as it was my first baby there was 'plenty of time'. *"You can go with the boat in the morning - first babies do not come as quickly as that"*. When my husband tried to insist that I be flown out, *"do not abuse the plane service"* was the answer he got. He was then told that, if a plane were indeed sent for, then it would be at our expense!

However, in the event, the doctor did decide to send me to Stobhill hospital as an 'emergency' (though still not by plane!) as I was three weeks early. Charlie McLean was thus detailed to take me by the Jura bus at 1.30 pm to Ardlussa at the north end of the island, as it was the New Year holiday and we had no ferries running. Once at Ardlussa we met Mrs Fletcher, whose private boat was going to take me over to Carsaig, where the ambulance would be waiting for me with one driver. Mrs Fletcher kindly offered to go with me if there were no one available; however, my mother had arrived the night before and was able to accompany me.

The road to Ardlussa

The doctor had said, *"If you get into any difficulties you can tell the ambulance man what to do, with you being a nurse."* However, I was in no fit state to do so! It was a terrible journey - even my mother was sick. I arrived at Stobhill Hospital at 9pm, where the doctor put me into the labour room right away as the baby's head was to be seen. Sheena was born at 9.40pm. She had turned in the ambulance, and so was born normally; however, we were told later that if she had been born in the ambulance itself she would quite possibly have died, as the cord was round her. When Alick got the news he phoned the doctor, who did not know what to say.

When I was having my second child Gordon I made sure I went away in good time!

On another occasion I haemorrhaged, and went again by boat, then by bus to Glasgow and train to Greenock. By then I was so exhausted that I took a taxi for the final stretch to Larkfield hospital. When I arrived, I was told that I should have been sent by plane.

I recount these experiences to let you see the difficulties we had in those days.

Working all hours

Nursing in those days, I was on twenty-four hour call, seven days a week, and not just for nursing care but also for 'last offices'. For all this I was paid the basic salary only, with no extra money for being called out. On the occasions when I did manage to have a holiday, my relief nurses came from far afield; Oban, Lochgilphead, Dunoon, or Carradale. My nursing officers were excellent and very understanding, and came to Islay hospital where we had meetings. Later, when Strathclyde took over from Oban I was taken on full time, working thirty-seven and a half hours a week, with the nurses from Islay covering days off and holidays, which made a great difference.

The Paps of Jura

Mary enjoying a short break!

In 1966 we had a very bad influenza epidemic, and quite a few of our elderly patients died. I was also laid up, but had to go back to work after a few days, as I had no relief nurse. I actually went back too soon, however, and I landed up at the county hospital in Oban as a patient myself, making the journey on the steamer from Jura pier as a foot passenger and being met at Tarbert by the ambulance. I was in hospital for two months with 'flu complications.

Babies galore!

Maternity cases could come in all shapes and sizes.

For instance, I had a call out one night to a case where a drunk had put his fist through the patient's window and startled her into labour. The doctor came too, and said that it would be quite a while before the birth. However, I thought differently, and indeed the baby arrived not long after the doctor had left. When he returned just a little later, we didn't let on immediately that the baby had arrived, so he was coming in to take a look, he thought, at just one patient. He didn't know what to say when I asked him whether he should be looking at the baby first! He was a very serious person, but took the joke in good part. Humour was quickly put aside, though, as our patient's condition started to deteriorate, with the placenta failing to come away properly and signs of shock starting to develop. We thus put up a drip, and it was arranged that a plane would stand by at Islay airport once it started to get light, as the passenger ferry at Feolin could not cross in the dark. Thankfully though, by the time daybreak came we had managed to sort out the complication. The plane was cancelled, and the patient was able to stay at home.

On another occasion I had a pregnant mother who had given birth to her previous baby up in the mountains in America. When she was expecting again I left a sterile maternity box with her in case it was needed before my arrival. She would not let a doctor see her. I had a call from her daughter at 9.30am to say that her mum had delivered at 5am, and that everything had been attended to before I arrived. I had to write out a report about it all and explain why I had left a maternity box with her since I was not at the birth.

When her next baby was due, I went up every day when she was near her time, in hopes of catching her at least in labour, but alas, one day I met the daughter at the top of the hill, who proclaimed *"I have a wee brother!"* She had done it again. They were always told to phone me, but they never did!

At another point, I accompanied our doctor's daughter-in-law, who was in labour, and was to be flown from Islay airport. However, when we arrived at Islay hospital and were waiting for the flight, the matron told us that it was now too late to go on the plane. *"Now that you are here, you can stay and deliver the baby,"* I was informed. Our patient duly had a lovely daughter, and when I got back to Jura I told the doctor that all had gone well - and that her granddaughter was her spitting image!

The ferry at Port Askaig

The time came when we were told not to deliver babies on the island, in case of any problems arising. But before that, of course, I had delivered many babies, and quite a number are still on the island!

In safe hands!

Bella

At one stage I was looking after a lady by the name of Bella; a great character, who was a diabetic on insulin. My relief nurse, who lived on Jura, went to see her one morning; Bella was obviously not in a very good mood, as she put the mop to the nurse's face and chased her away! Fortunately, the nurse managed to calm her down and got on with her treatment.

I got on very well with Bella, and on one of my days off I took my mother to meet her, and recorded her singing. She went on for a whole hour; it was like a ceilidh, with talking and clapping in between. She was very good, and both her husband and my mother enjoyed it greatly. When I played it back to her, she was amazed at hearing her own voice. One of the songs was a funny one. *"Don't let the minister hear that one."* she said as it finished. I still have that tape of her singing to this day.

I remember one morning going up to give Bella her insulin. I knocked on the door, and had a job getting any response. Her husband eventually answered, and said that his wife was still sleeping. Worried, I rushed through to the bedroom; as I suspected, Bella was in a coma. I called the doctor, and we both worked on Bella, and brought her round. We then arranged for her to be admitted to hospital in Oban. For this, we had to hire a Land Rover to take us to Feolin Ferry, as it was snowing.

A wintry Keills!

Not long afterwards, at a meeting in Islay Hospital, I happened to meet the specialist from Oban. I asked how Bella was keeping, and he started to smile. *"I went over to see her on my rounds to ask how she was,"* he told me, *"and the reply was, don't bother me just now, I'm listening to a Gaelic ceilidh on the wireless, come back later!"*

That is the character Bella was. Until she died I brought in her coal, did her messages and got her pension. I also wrote letters for her, as she would not have a home help and she lived a long way from the village, with no neighbour beside her. She was a great person and so was her husband. He, at one time, fell into a drain where he had been fixing the water to the house. Two stalkers out shooting found him. He was taken to his son's house until he went to hospital, suffering from hypothermia. He was an elderly man, but he survived where many a younger person would have died.

All in a day's work ...

Nursing life was never dull!

At one point, I had to attend to a patient every day to change a dressing. She lived a long distance up the island, and one particular day there had been a very heavy fall of snow, leaving that part of Jura virtually cut off. As I only had a small car I could only get up the island so far, so I phoned the person who dealt with the cars at the Vale of Leven hospital, who was not very helpful. Was it really necessary, he asked, for me to go up the island every day? I told him that if it were not necessary I would not be going up, so he let me hire a Land Rover. My car had no four-wheel drive; again, you can see the difficulties we often had.

Evacuation of patients from Jura to hospital on the mainland often required the patient to be escorted, and I accompanied quite a few patients in my time, by ferry, and by lifeboat too when the weather was rough. At one stage, we had a bad outbreak of Salmonella, and one of my patients, who was a schoolboy, had to be taken over to Islay to catch the plane, and then on to Ruchill Hospital. Fortunately he recovered safely and returned home.

The Islay lifeboat on standby at Port Askaig

In those days we had no weekend home help service, which meant that when you were attending a patient who was confined to bed on Saturdays or Sundays, you made her breakfast and put on her fire after seeing to her nursing needs. As well as being a Nurse you were also a friend.

In the same way, one day I was nursing up at the north end of the island, when my husband had a phone call from two elderly ladies, who lived near us, to ask if I would go and see them. When I came home, I went down and asked whether they were they all right. *"Oh yes,"* one said, *"we just wanted you to lift the pots off the fire for us."* This I duly did and went home.

During my time nursing, if someone died, we had to perform the last offices, as we had no one else to do this. The undertaker was in Islay, and we only had the passenger ferry, so no way of bringing the hearse over. Dougie Buie did all the measuring and ordered the coffins. At that time, when people were buried, the hearse would often be a Land Rover, or some other conveyance that could cope with the terrain, unlike today, when everything is done through Islay to Jura.

On one occasion, we had a crowd of officials flying in to meet Dr. Garrett and myself, and to see the island. The plane was due to land at Corran beach, where we had an emergency air strip, but they couldn't land as the airstrip was full of cattle, so they had to circle until the cattle were moved off. On board the plane there was a photographer who took photos and said it was just like a rodeo!

Air Ambulance at Corran airstrip

On another occasion I was called out to a patient with chest pains. After seeing my patient I had to contact the doctor. Unfortunately, though, she was up at the north end of the island as it was Ardlussa Sports Day, and she was going to be presenting the prizes. I tried the phone, but the line was continuously engaged, so I called my relief nurse to sit with my patient while I motored up to Ardlussa, which was roughly twenty miles, and told the doctor what had happened. We both came down straight away. An ambulance was called, and the Air Ambulance was laid on to land at our airstrip at Corran sands. While taking our patient to the airstrip, I got the ambulance to stop as the patient was hardly breathing. The doctor was right behind me so I called for her, and she treated the patient. We carried on to the airstrip, where the Air Ambulance plane was waiting. The patient was taken to Glasgow, and in fact there was a happy ending, as the patient survived.

The telephone exchange phoned us later to say that children had been playing on the phone!

Once we were called to a patient who had chest pains and was also diabetic. The doctor decided not to move the patient, but rather to wait forty-eight hours to see how things went. It was believed at that time that if you left the patient for this period it would give him or her a chance to rest, be treated and recover. Fortunately our patient did indeed recover, and we were able to keep him at home.

At another point, one of the two elderly ladies who lived near me had a bad nose bleed. I was having my day off, and she would not let the relief nurse near her, so that nurse asked me to go down with her. I packed the lady's nose, knowing the technique from my two years as Senior Sister in the Ear Nose and Throat Hospital in Greenock. The patient did eventually let the relief nurse attend to her!

On another of my days off, another neighbour had pains in his chest. The relief nurse attended to him, but on my way home the doctor stopped me, and asked if I would go and see my neighbour. I went to him with my relief nurse. The patient asked if I would gather a few things together for him to take with him to hospital, as I knew where everything was. When the ambulance arrived, he refused to go on a stretcher, and demanded to walk on. Unfortunately he died a few days later in hospital. His brother was devastated when we told him his brother had died, as they had lived together for years.

The ferry approaching Craighouse pier

A ceilidh to remember

I continued my nursing until July 1993, when both my husband and I became ill. Due to these health problems, I retired in November of that year. The community gave me a lovely retiral ceilidh, at which I was presented with a teasmade and cheque by Charlie McLean. Dr Garrett and Charlie both made lovely speeches. A lot of my nursing colleagues came over from Islay, including Miss McKinnon, who was the Matron in Islay Hospital, and who retired in the same year as myself. Dr. and Mrs McDonald were also present.

Mary receiving retirement gifts from Charlie Maclean

Sheena, my daughter, and Cheryl, my granddaughter from Jersey, and my two other grandchildren, Kirsten and Duncan from Lennoxtown, all came to support me for the occasion. Sheena also made a lovely speech and sang for me. It was a lovely evening. Winnie McDonald presented me with a bouquet of flowers. It was sad leaving, but I knew I could not carry on any longer. I knew I would miss the role, but as I said in my speech, like the joiner, who has, at some point, to lay down his tools, I knew the time had come to lay mine down too. And so that was the end of my nursing career of thirty and a half years, during which I was very happy to serve and help you all.

Mary Keith

District Nursing Sister/Midwife - RGN/SCM

2009

I would like to thank everyone for the lovely gifts, cheques and cards, flowers given to me on my retirement, also the ceilidh they held for me, and to thank Dr. Garrett, Charlie McLean, for the speeches and kind remarks about me, also my husband Alick's present. I would also like to thank the Hospital Staff and District Sisters in Islay Hospital for the lovely evening they gave to Alick and myself, also for the lovely gift, also to thank Argyll and Clyde Health Board for the gift of money to me, much appreciated. Wishing you all a very happy New Year.

MARY KEITH

Mrs Mary Keith's Retirement Ceilidh

A good time was had by all when family, friends and colleagues gathered to wish Mrs Keith a long and happy retirement. Dr Garrett expressed the thanks for Mary's 30 years of faithful and caring service. He personally appreciated the fact that on his coming to Jura he found one Nurse who could competently carry out the duties of three - Midwife, District Nurse and Health Visitor.

Charlie Maclean, on behalf of the community, presented Mary with a 'Teasmade' and a cheque, a bouquet of flowers was presented by Winnie MacDonald.

Following the 'retirement toast', Mary warmly thanked all who had contributed towards her gifts and those who had organised the evening. After she had cut her retirement cake, tea, coffee and a splendid selection of teas were enjoyed by the assembled company.

A varied programme of instrumental music, dancing and songs in Gaelic and English, compered by Gordon Wright, entertained the gathering.

Donald Ewen Darroch summed up the evening in an ably expressed comprehensive vote of thanks.

Mary and Alick, you are wished very many happy years of retirement, with plenty of morning 'cuppas' in bed.

From the 'Ileach'

List of colleagues

Doctors:

Dr McIntyre,   Dr Robertson

Dr Taylor,   Dr Johnson

Dr Garrett,   Dr Acres

Medical Officers of Health, Oban (my employers):

Dr Allan,   Dr Watters

Nursing Officers:

Miss Stewart

Mrs McIntosh (Lochgilphead)

Mrs Girvan (Campbeltown)

Miss McKinnon (Islay)

Miss Drummond (Campbeltown)

Jura Relief Nurses:

Betty Bateman   Ruth Stead

Catherine Robertson

Acknowledgements

Reproduction of photographs: Iain Colborn

Aeroplane photograph: Dr Stewart Garrett

Editing and layout: Moray and Janet Grigor

With Alick

Postscript

I was down in the hotel several years ago and got chatting to a lady who said she had not been in Jura for twenty years. I asked if she was on holiday, and she told me that in fact her family owned one of the estates. I realised right away that she must be the lady laird that I had attended all those years ago. She told me that she had been trying to find out if the District Nurse she knew was still living in Jura; I was able to confirm that she was indeed! She was delighted that we had met up again, and we had a long chat. As she left, she took a picture to show her daughter the nurse who had helped to save her. It *is* a small world!

With the family